Table of Contents

Illustrations

Page

"The nature of the Iranian regime, not the power of nuclear weapons, makes a nuclear Iran a threat to the United States." - Dr. Douglas Streusand[1]

The mysterious nuclear weapons program of the Islamic Republic of Iran has perplexed the entire world. While the United States (U.S.) is one of the countries most ardently against the program, U.S. politicians have remained virtually silent without instituting any compelling or constructive diplomatic efforts. The United States' invasion and subsequent disassembling of Iran's only counterbalance, Saddam Hussein and his Ba'athist government, give Iran full entitlements as the local hegemon due to its strategic geographic size, location, and immense population. Diplomatic idleness towards Iran and overzealous actions in Iraq give Iran freedom and time to complete its nuclear ambitions, thus becoming the second nuclear armed country in the Middle East after Israel. Iran's sponsorship of terrorist organizations and threat to dismantle Israel make a nuclear armed Iran intolerable. However, time is drawing towards this realization. Iranian President Mahmoud Ahmadinejad has already declared victory for Iran's nuclear program following a 2007 National Intelligence Estimate (NIE) that declared "Tehran halted its nuclear weapons programs" in 2003. The Director of National Intelligence, Admiral Michael McConnell, has since attempted to elucidate the declaration by stating Iran's nuclear weapons program, as defined by the NIE, includes only design and weaponization and does **_not_** include uranium enrichment.[2] The confusion over these two end states proves a lack of understanding and intelligence on Iran which has not occurred since the 1979 Islamic Republic takeover by Ruhollah Khomeini and the subsequent detention of 52 U.S. hostages for 444 days. The United States must take immediate non-military action in an attempt to end Iran's nuclear weapons ambitions and its indirect support of globalized terrorism through proxy fundamentalist groups. U.S. politicians must first engage in diplomacy. If Iran fails to cooperate, the U.S. should then recognize and capitalize upon Iran's internal challenges through an aggressive and relentless information operations campaign. This paper will examine Iran's internal challenges to include quandaries with the Iranian people, politics, and plateau and will recommend actions the United States government must take to capitalize on these challenges in an attempt to change Iran's strategic endeavors.

People

The demography of Iran's population contains a varied mixture of cultures. There are over 65 million Iranian citizens with a slight majority, 51%, coming from the native Persian culture. A variety of other ethnic backgrounds are represented by Azeri (24%); Gilaki and Mazandarani (8%); Kurd (7%); Arab (3%); Lur (2%); Baloch (2%); and, Turkmen (2%) lineage (1% of Iranians come from and are classified as "other").[3] Iran's diverse population continues to be the subject of government oppression as it has been since the establishment of the Islamic Regime in 1979. Ruhollah Musawi Khomeini, the creator and first Supreme Leader of the Islamic Republic of Iran, wrote in 1941 concerning the government under newly crowned monarch Reza Shah Pahlavi:

> When a government does not perform its duty, it becomes oppressive. If it does not perform its duty, not only is it not oppressive, it is cherished and honored by God. The duty of government, therefore, must be in order for us to establish whether the present government is oppressive or not. …In short, these idiotic and treacherous rulers, these officials – high and low – these reprobates and smugglers must change in order for the country to change. Otherwise, you will experience worse times that these, times so bad that the present will seem like a paradise by comparison.[4]

The statement presents two facts concerning the fundamental beliefs of Khomeini: 1) Islamic law is truly a way for all people, regardless of religion or ethnicity, to enjoy the inherent freedoms of Islamic law; and 2) Shah Pahlavi's monarchy is extremely oppressive.

Current Iranian circumstances indicate Khomeini's rhetoric from 1941 to 1979 was a stratagem to garner support for himself and for his vision of a theocracy. Today, the Islamic government established by Khomeini is more oppressive than at any time during Pahlavi's 37-year rule. In response, Iranian citizens from all backgrounds are coming together to display their resentment towards current leaders concerning freedoms and liberties promised by Khomeini and his new Islamic Republic.

Khomeini never intended for Iran's new government to allow its people full independence. Freedoms, in the form of speech, assembly, women's and political rights are controlled by President Ahmadinejad just as they were in 1979 under Khomeini. However, unlike the early years under Khomeini where nationalism and symbolism abounded -- especially after the 1980 invasion of Iran by Iraq -- increased demonstrations by the youth movement have created a greater challenge for officials in Iran.

Sixty percent, or two-thirds of the population of Iran, are less than 30 years of age, and eighty-six percent of the population is literate.[5] The explosive combination of oppression, education, and youth, combined with curiosities witnessed as a result of globalization (e.g., internet, movies) is creating havoc for current government officials similar to that of uprisings against the Pahlavi regime in 1979.

Iranian citizens have often organized to demonstrate their opposition against past and present Iranian government policies and leaders. The first ruling Pahlavi, Reza Shah, implemented several changes to Iran's Arab-influenced civilization, including dispensing with traditional religious ceremonies that impressed on the people his reliance on the mullahs for religious legitimacy to his dynasty. Reza Shah also implemented several European-style characteristics including a change in traditional male attire, a clean-shaven face to denounce religious connotations, and a requirement for women to stop wearing the traditional chador. The Shah ensured compliance with the new rules by ordering military officers to severely punish women and mullahs who did not abide by the new laws.[6] He continued to eliminate Arabic influences and diminish mullah authority to a point where nationalism became incompatible with Iranian clerics including then-Hojjatoleslam Ruhollah Khomeini.

Mohammad Reza Pahlavi continued his father's quest to stimulate Iranian secular nationalism with an increased assistance and recognizable influence from the United States. The younger Pahlavi, however, made several bizarre efforts during his reign from 1941 – 1979, that would enrage Iranian citizens and mullahs, thereby reversing his intended effects. For example, he declared himself an heir to Cyrus the Great (founder of the Persian Empire) and changed the Iranian calendar to start at the beginning of the Achaemenian dynasty. The most eccentric effort was a 1971 party to celebrate the 2,500th anniversary of the Iranian monarchy at a cost of $100 million.[7] By the end of Reza Shah Pahlavi's rule, the prideful Persian nation of Iran was in economic ruin and its people severely oppressed. The synthesis of Western influences and restriction of liberties was a deadly combination for Pahlavi and allowed Ruhollah Khomeini, a symbolic figurehead of Islamic change, to lead a revolutionary metamorphosis in Iran.

Resistance to the Shah intensified in the streets of Tehran and on September 8th, 1978, also known as "Black Friday." Thousands of protestors took to the streets of Tehran to peacefully demonstrate against the Shah, who responded by declaring Martial Law. Soldiers took aim and shot at the thousands of protestors, killing 88 people, 64 of whom were in Jaleh Square.[8] Most, if not all, protests were under the auspices of Khomeini while he was exiled in Iraq then Paris, were he was preparing for his return to Iran.

Students continue to effectively demonstrate their displeasure with the current regime, albeit through smaller protests than Khomeini was able to direct. For example, hundreds of Polytechnic University students demonstrated during a speech by President Ahmadinejad in December 2006, in response to his repressiveness on individual freedoms, poor economic policies, and abrasive rhetoric towards the West. Protestors were further enraged when buses of Ahmadinejad supporters arrived at the University before the presidential speech as staged support for the president. Students shouted "death to the dictator" and interrupted him several times during his speech; they were also successful in shortening both his speech and his stay at the University.[9] Furthermore, on December 4, 2007, 250 students demonstrated at Tehran University chanting "freedom and equality" and "no to war" in response to Ahmadinejad's threat to the West concerning nuclear weapons. Similar protests broke out in other cities of Iran including Hamadan, Isfahan, Mazandaran, Shiraz, and Kerman. Twenty students were arrested and, while most were released, a few remain inside Evin prison along with at least one other student demonstrator from 1999.

There is likely no end to these demonstrations and they will likely increase in the months leading to the presidential election of 2009.[10] December is a month commonly filled with student demonstrations marking the anniversary of Student Day. Three students were killed by police as they protested then-Vice President Nixon's visit to Iran on December 6, 1953.[11] While many student demonstration unions exist in Iran, the unions still lack organization and a strong leader to guide them towards any major policy or regime change as Khomeini did leading up to the Islamic Revolution of 1979.

Many citizens of Iran believed Ahura Pirouz Khaleghi Yazdi was the man who could lead them in changing the Iranian regime. Yazdi, a resident of Northern Virginia and born of an

Iranian father and Kurdish mother, promised to liberate the Iranian people upon his return along with 50 aircraft and 2000 supporters on October 1, 2004. Through a simple three-month campaign aired through inexpensive satellite television and internet websites, Yazdi promised regime change, freedom of speech, women's rights, freedom of the press, and freedom of religion. The news of Yazdi's return was published in several articles, from BBC News to *The Washington Post,* and several (illegal) internet blog sites were filled with enthusiasm concerning the arrival of their liberator to Iran.

On the day of his proposed arrival, thousands of anxious demonstrators took to the streets and peacefully cheered for Yazdi's return.[12] However, Yazdi and his supporters never arrived. In fact, he never had plans to return. After postponing his first "arrival" to Iran, he later announced his intention to permanently postpone his return because of threats made on his life (which were fabricated by Yazdi). Yazdi's acts were deceitful and devious and gave false hope to thousands of Iranians. Nevertheless, the endeavor proved three important points: 1) the ease of gaining inexpensive access to Iranians through satellite television, 2) the effects external influences have upon the people of Iran, and, 3) the Iranian appetite for a symbolic leader to topple the current form of government and its leaders.

Yazdi's rhetoric was introduced to Iranians through an inexpensive satellite television transmission from Virginia. Rang-A-Rang, a Persian language production company located in Vienna, Virginia, infiltrates Iranian televisions and reaches a self-proclaimed 80 million people in Iran. Founded in 1989 by Davar Veiseh, the 24-hour satellite channel criticizes the Iranian government and its officials and debunks propaganda efforts by the government usually aimed at the U.S. Satellite antennas are often physically removed by Basij forces, a volunteer force founded by the Ayatollah Khomeini in 1979 used to enforce Islamic law and protect the Islamic

Republic. Satellite television was banned in Iran in 1994; however, Iran has an estimated 3 – 4 million satellite television viewers and it is not strictly enforced.[13] Veisah hopes to reach these viewers and influence the upcoming 2009 Presidential elections and ultimately would like to see a complete regime change.

Iranian youth have the ability to influence elections at every level if the elections are honest throughout the entire process. Interest and participation in elections are highest among the youth of Iran and slowly declines with age.[14] Unlike in the United States, where the minimum voting age is 18, Iran's minimum voting age was 15, until January 2007, when parliament changed it to 18.[15] The youth vote (i.e., less than 20 years of age) is essential as the majority group within Iran. There is a growing frustration within various movements within Iran, many of which involve the youth movement, caused by the Islamic Republic's oppressive demands.

Iranian youth were identified as key players in the march, 2008 parliamentary elections, a harbinger for the early-to mid-2009 Presidential elections. As expected by Iranian scholars and Iranian youth, election results favored pro-Ahmadinejad hard-line conservatives. Iran's main student opposition group, Islamic Iran's Organization of the Educated Ones, made a statement concerning whether they vote or not that "The elections have been engineered in a way that it doesn't matter how many people participate. Either way, more conservative members will enter parliament."[16]

Meanwhile, Iranian propaganda paints another picture and credits the youth by stating, "The massive turnout and energetic participation of overwhelmingly young people in Iran's election shows that the new round of United Nations Security Council sanctions and massive U.S. anti-Iran propaganda beamed at the youth of Iran did not affect the nation's clarity of purpose."[17] Propaganda from government-controlled newspapers, radio, and internet sites continue to present false information in an attempt to save the Islamic Republic from reformist preservation and infiltration. As a matter of fact, over 100 independent media outlets have been closed in recent years, including newspapers and Web sites; and those specifically dealing with women, minority, and religious rights have been further suppressed. In addition, Ahmadinejad recently established a "societal-security project" to protect the population against robbers, criminals, pickpockets, thieves, and urban violence. The program's real reason for existence is to restrict Iranian rights from expressions of what the government defines as "immoral" and to re-establish societal norms as they were in the Khomeini era.[18]

In a recent example of how the new Islamic Guidance Units function, agents attempted to arrest a young Iranian girl for simply walking beside her boyfriend in Tehran. The girl resisted arrest and was subsequently beaten by the agents until she was immobilized and bleeding. Several bystanders intervened on her behalf and prevented the agents from taking her into custody. More people arrived and what started as a few bystanders turned into several hundred demonstrators who chanted, "We don't want dictatorship," "We don't want emergency and martial law."[19] The courage to stand against abusive, coercive, and controlling forces at the risk of physical punishment, imprisonment, and death are indicative of the level of frustration citizens have with the government.

Many people inside Iran are also beginning to adopt many Western culture characteristics. Even though the Iranian Government bans Western television shows, music, and internet sites, such as MySpace, Face Book, and You Tube, many of these illegal media venues are accessible because technical errors on some black market channels and Internet sites prevent them from being blocked. As a result, the youth "rebel" by participating in and taking on Western characteristics inside Iran to include women pulling their headscarves back to reveal more of their hair, listening to Western music, wearing heavy makeup and Western hairstyles, and physically touching the opposite sex in public.[20] While rebelling against oppressive Iranian governments may not be new, the increase and severity of incidents (with distinguishing Western characteristics) are distinctly different.

Politics

The complex political structure of the Iranian theocratic government is unique compared to other world governments. Khomeini returned to Iran on February 1, 1979 and established an Islamic Republic on April 1, 1979 (see Appendix A). A new government based on Islam and Islamic law (Sharia) was formed as the foundation for the new government, and the constitutional authority of the government was granted to the valet-e faqih (rule of jurors) and leader of the revolution, the Supreme Leader.[21] Little internal opposition towards the oppressive government existed until the mid-1990s, when several political parties emerged to challenge the traditional Islamic regime. The only exception, and major armed opposition to the Islamic Regime was the Mujahadeen-e-Khalq (MEK).

The MEK was founded in the 1960s by educated youth opposed to Reza Shah Pahlavi and was the most militant group opposed to the Islamic Republic following the takeover by Khomeini in 1979. As a result of ideological differences between the MEK and the new government, several MEK leaders were executed, forcing the group to flee to Paris. The MEK has denounced violence since 2001, and has reformed as The National Council of Resistance of Iran (NCRI); however, it still remains on the U.S. Department of State's Terrorist Organization List, where it has been since 1997.[22] A woman and co-founder of the MEK, Maryam Rajavi, is currently president-elect of the NCRI. The NCRI proclaims to be the democratic parliament-inexile and boasts about its minority representation and rights, including women who make up half of its members.[23]

In a telephone poll conducted in June of 2007, by Terror Free Tomorrow, an overwhelming majority (i.e., 79%) favored a democracy where the people elect all leaders, including the Supreme Leader, are elected by the people. Currently, the people elect the parliament (i.e., legislative branch) and president (i.e., executive branch), and the Assembly of Experts appoints the Supreme Leader for life. In addition, when asked about the overall economic situation in Iran today, an overwhelming 79.7% stated that it was either fair or poor, and 75.2% said that their own personal financial situation was either the same or worse, than it was when President Ahmadinejad took office in August 2005. When asked if the pollster either favored or opposed investment from Western countries in Iran to create more jobs, 74.8% favored or somewhat favored the idea and while 20.9% opposed or strongly opposed the idea.[24] The results of the poll indicate the Iranian people's concerns about the failure of the political situation in Iran and its economic decline.

The balance of power built into the Iranian government by the Constitution ensures a single person or group does not have absolute power. Yet, President Ahmadinejad's travel to Iraq and the United States, threats of nuclear weapons' proliferation and destruction of Israel may create a belief that he is the sole source of power and decision-maker within Iran. In fact, his presidential powers only extend to social, cultural, and economic policies of Iran and not foreign policy. Additionally, Ahmadinejad is the second most powerful figurehead in Iran behind the Supreme Leader: and the assembly, which has the authority to remove the president with a two-thirds majority no-confidence vote, has the power to keep him in check.[25]

The Supreme Leader, Ayatollah Ali Khamene'i, actually is the authority to oversee Iranian foreign and domestic affairs, including the command of Iranian armed forces. In accordance with Article 107 of the 1979 constitution, the position of supreme leader is selected by the Assembly of Experts, and it is a position held for life. Khamene'i, a conservative who displays a variation of conservative tendencies to maintain the status quo, assumed his position upon the death of Khomeini in 1989.

Khamene'i's adverse relationship and dissatisfaction with past presidential nominees are beginning to permeate into the Ahmadinejad camp. While initially supporting Ahmadinejad's agenda to alleviate poverty, unemployment, and corruption, Khamene'i and other clergy members have distanced themselves from Ahmadinejad since his election in June 2005. Since then, Ahmadinejad has isolated not only his country from the rest of the world, but also isolated himself from his own political allies. As president, he has failed to improve the economy and has not brought "the fruits of Iran's oil wealth to the dinner table of every Iranian home", but has increased the elite status and decreasing Iranian liberties.[26] His actions and rhetoric to have Israel "wiped off the map," his ambition to pave the way for the reappearance of the 12th Imam, the Mahdi (which includes a world filled with oppression and tyranny), isolationism, and threats to obtain nuclear weaponry may be too hard-lined even for Khamene'i.[27] In response, Khamene'i has expressed dissatisfaction with Ahmadinejad as witnessed in two recent public examples. In January 2008, Ayatollah Khamene'i publicly reprimanded President Ahmadinejad for objecting to the Majles reverse decision *not* to close several economic institutions and for changing the time of summer and winter in Iran as Ahmadinejad mandated.[28] This dispute is an example of how Ahmadinejad is isolating himself from fellow party members; and 156 of the 290-members of the Majles, or 54%, are conservative.

Recent changes in formal party leadership within the Iranian political system may reveal an upcoming and historic change to the political elite. On September 4, 2007, Ali Akbar Rafsanjani was elected as the new Assembly of Experts speaker. As mentioned earlier, the Assembly of Experts is responsible for electing the Supreme Leader and has the responsibility to remove the Supreme Leader if warranted by the assembly. Rafsanjani was president of Iran from 1989 to 1997 and was in firm control of Iran when Khamene'i took over as Supreme Leader in 1989. However, after three years as Supreme Leader, Khamene'i finally established a stronghold over Rafsanjani and forced traditionalist right leaders into Rafsanjani's modern right organization. Harsh feelings toward each other were the norm and re-escalated during the 2005 Presidential election in which Rafsanjani lost to Ahmadinejad. Rafsanjani and other presidential candidates documented several allegations of election manipulation. When asked why a complaint was not made, Rafsanjani stated, "The people who are supposed to deal with these violations are the same who have committed them," referring to and implying that Khamene'i was responsible for the election outcome.[29]

Parliamentary elections are usually a precursor for the presidential elections. In the 2004 Parliamentary elections, several events took place that turned the dominate reformist parliament into the dominate conservative parliament. First, conservatives within the Majles blocked Reformists' efforts to implement political and social reforms called upon by then President Khatami, leaving Iranian citizens frustrated with empty promises by Khatami. Second, Conservatives saw an opportunity to win votes by advocating a change in conservative thinking to the "China Model." This model consists of four main elements: 1) reforming Iran's economy by reducing unemployment, 2) more liberal dress codes and other easing of restrictions on women, 3) better relations with the West (including the United States), 4) and the least mentioned, restrictions on and suppression of challengers of the Islamic regime and its conservative leaders. A third event that occurred was the Guardian Council disqualified 43% (an overwhelming amount of reformist candidates) of the over 8,000 registered candidates, leaving a very limited number of the reformist candidates available for voters to elect.[30] Politics in Iran is a very complex system with an unscrupulous checks-and-balances system; all checks are written by the Supreme Leader as long as they balance towards the sustainment of the Islamic regime.

In January 2008, 7,200 candidates registered to run for one of 290 seats in parliament. Initially, over 2,000 candidates were eliminated by the Council of Guardians, a group of 12 jurists (six members are appointed by the Supreme Leader and six members are appointed by the Majles from nominees selected by the head of the judiciary, also appointed by the Supreme Leader) responsible for vetting electoral candidates based on the candidates' Islamic loyalty.[31] Several complaints from the reformist camp, and some from the conservative camp, allowed the Guardian Council to reconsider some of the 2000 candidates initially rejected. Of these, 831 candidates were reinstated, including the founder of the Islamic regimes grandson, Seyyed Hassan Khomeini, and former Iranian president Mohammad Khatami.[32]

Plateau

A plateau is defined as a land area having a "relatively flat surface considerably raised above adjoining land on a least one side and often cut by deep canyons."[33] Iran's flatland is partially surrounded by the Elburz Mountains that extend for nearly 400 miles from the Northwest to the Northeast, withholding a 15-mile wide fertile area that lies between the Caspian Sea and the mountain range. The Zagros Mountains extend for nearly 1,000 miles from the Northwest to the Southwest and nearly block off Iran's plateau from the Strait of Hormuz to the Northern Turkish border (see Appendix B).[34] As noted earlier, several ethnicities exist within Iran and live in groups in sections within Iran's borders (see Appendix C). With the first priority of the Islamic Regime relying on the Islamic Republic's survival, the next goal is the survival of Iran proper. Iranian leadership is concerned that the United States will not stop at regime change, but will continue its conquest and change the physical borders of Iran. Ralph Peters outlines one concept of redrawing the border in an *Armed Forces Journal* article. In *Blood Borders*, Peters asserts "a more peaceful Middle East" would exist if current political borders were redrawn to encompass major ethnic groups.[35] Iran would lose much of its territory in the Northwest, West, and Southeast, including mountainous areas containing much of Iran's oil reserve and gain territory from a predominantly Persian populated area of Afghanistan (see Appendix D). The thought of redrawing the Iranian border is not a Bush administration goal, nor would Iran accept it if it were. The last time a country (Iraq) made a border demand on Iran, the countries fought an eight-year war at a cost of over one million lives.

Iran's majority of oil comes from the Zagros Mountain area from Lali to Gachsaran (see Appendix E) and accounts for much of the four million barrels per day (bbl/day) produced by Iran. Iran exports 2.52 bbl/day and is responsible for 90% of Iran's export earnings, making it the second largest exporter in the world. Likewise, Iran imports about 43% of its petroleum from 16 countries, including the United Arab Emirates, India, the Netherlands, and France.[36] The reason for the high rate of oil imports is the lack of an oil refinery capacity and an amazing 70 million liter per day petroleum use, approximately the same amount consumed by China (China has a population that is 18 times larger than Iran's.)[37]

Iran has the capability to refine 44 million liters of petroleum each day, approximately 62% of its daily domestic requirement. Iran currently has nine refineries and plans to expand current refinery operations at six of these totaling 350,000 bpd at six of its refineries.[38] Iran also plans on cooperating by providing crude oil to five international refineries in China, Singapore, Malaysia, Indonesia, and Syria in return for refined oil. These five sites can produce 1.1 billion barrels of refined oil per day.[39] Iran has also announced plans to invest money (and likely crude oil) in Zimbabwe's Feruka Oil Refinery, which can produce 10,000 barrels per day (bpd). Iran assisted in building the refinery in 1965, before it was shut down after one year due to a petroleum embargo to (then) Rhodesia.[40]

Iran shares borders with seven countries: Azerbaijan, Armenia, Turkmenistan, Turkey, Iraq, Pakistan, and Afghanistan. The last two countries are the biggest producers of drugs imported into Iran, the Middle East, and Europe. In 2004, 53% of the world's record high 59.2 tons of seized heroin passed through Iran enroute to its European destinations (see Appendix F). [41] In 2006, Afghanistan alone produced 6,100 tons of heroin, 80% of which flowed through the porous borders of Iran, while only one-quarter of the heroin was intercepted by border police. Iran has an estimated three million drug users (some place the estimate at seven million) and the worst heroin addiction rate in the world. Unemployment and availability are key factors why most of the addicts are Iran's youth, primarily within the 22 to 33 age group. The wealthy entertain drug usage from sheer boredom.[42]

Heavily armed drug convoys escort the illegal drugs into Iran from Afghanistan using armed violence to protect the drugs and the people's way of life. In a 27-year period from 1979 – 2006, 3,600 Iranian border police were killed during clashes with criminals escorting drugs into Iran.[43] Meanwhile, the Iranian government is blamed for allowing gangs to traffic large quantities of drugs through Iran for information that leads to the arrest and seizure of other would-be traffickers. Ali Hashemi, the former head of the Drugs Control Headquarters, admitted that some officials have been involved in trafficking, although no official has ever been charged.[44]

Response

Washington policymakers' refusal of international diplomacy with the Islamic Republic of Iran has allowed the country to escalate its nuclear enrichment program. President Bush and his administration have made it clear that everything will be done to ensure that Iran does not procure nuclear weapons, including re-considering the grand bargain offered to the United States in 2003 by Iran. As the largest state sponsor of terrorism with close ties to Hizbollah, Hamas, and Islamic terrorist groups around the world, there is little doubt that the current Iranian administration would confront its foes by proxy through terrorists armed with nuclear devices.

Diplomatic policy attempts need to be direct with Supreme Leader Khamene'i to further isolate President Ahmadinejad and others within the Islamic Republic administration. Certainly all contact with Ahmadinejad must be avoided due to his anti-Western rhetoric and his lack of foreign policy authority. His rhetoric concerning the destruction of Israel and facilitating the return of the 12th Imam has distanced himself from his own party members making it easier for the U.S. to influence Iranians to do the same. In the past, Khamene'i has limited his contact with Western diplomats, instead sending representatives with absolutely no authority to make foreign policy decisions which remain with Khamene'i. All attempts to contact Khamene'i should be highly publicized including his response to the efforts, informing the American and Iranian citizens on the level of effort the U.S. is putting into resolving present day issues.

President Bush can no longer "isolate" Iran only through economic embargos. He must diplomatically engage Iranian leaders in an all-out attempt to increase relations with Iran and stop its nuclear ambitions. Further denial of diplomacy will ultimately lead to Iran's acquirement if nuclear weapons, ultimately requiring military force that the United States is not ready to administer.

The United States is not in a position to take the offensive and militarily engage Iran for two reasons. *First*, there is deficient intelligence concerning the exact number and location of specific nuclear-related targets. The lack of human intelligence inside Iran since the hostile Islamic Republic has placed the U.S. at a disadvantage. If, only as a last resort, a military option was to occur, U.S. warplanes and Naval vessels would have to use an abundant amount of firepower to destroy all underground nuclear sites causing an extensive amount of collateral damage and civilian casualties. This scenario would create the opposite effect of the desired citizen disposition towards the U.S. (frustration and resentment) and towards the Iranian government (increased support). A sense of nationalism would overcome Iran's citizens as it did when Iraq, who by all accounts should have defeated Iran, invaded Iran in September 1980. *Second*, the nationalism and resentful attitude towards the U.S. would delay the desired political endstate of Iran, the end of its Islamic regime. (See Major William Lee's paper entitled *Iranian Nationalism: How Military Action in Iran will Prolong the Regime*).

The Bush administration failed to accept an exceptional proposal from Iran following the 2003 invasion of Iraq. In President Bush's January 2002 State of the Union address, he labeled Iran, North Korea, and Iraq as states that formed an "Axis of Evil."[45] Then, on March 20, 2003, the Americans, along with smaller contingents of friendly forces, invaded Iran's neighbor Iraq. By May 1, 2003, the coalition forces swiftly defeated Iraqi forces, a feat the Iranians could not accomplish after eight years of bloody and costly war. Fearing for his regime's survival, Supreme Leader Khamene'i agreed to several conditions: to stop all support of opposition groups, such as Hamas, and pressure the groups to cease violence inside Israel; pressure Hizbollah to become a political organization; accept the Arab League declaration formally recognizing and consider itself at peace with Israel; promote stabilization in Iraq; apply decisive action against all terrorist groups within the borders of Iran; and finally the most prolific agreement, to completely

open Iran's nuclear endeavors for inspection by the IAEA. In return, Iran asked for a halt in U.S.

hostile behavior towards Iran ("axis of evil" and terrorism list); eliminate all sanctions including

international trade and financial assets; respect for Iranian interests in Iraq; recognition of Iran's

security concerns in the area; pursue MEK and anti-Iranian terrorists; and rights to full access to

peaceful nuclear, bio, and chemical technology. This proposal was the deal of the millennium.[46]

To the world's astonishment, to the perplexity and shock of everyone involved, President Bush

and former Secretary of Defense Donald Rumsfeld rejected the proposal. The president never

passed a formal response to Iran stating, "We don't speak to evil."[47]

The United States must come to diplomatic terms with Iran before it is too late. Diplomatic

and further economic exchanges should start immediately with an intense informational

operation concentrated on Iranian leadership and citizens while saturating U.S. media outlets

with Iranian acts of oppression and America's new attempt to resolve peacefully the nuclear

crisis. U.S.-sponsored media, such as Radio Farda and the Voice of America, already exist

inside Iran, however, they need a complete overhaul to rebuild credibility and reach more

Iranians. Specifically, monetary, managerial, and recruiting problems have plagued both outlets,

which have not been particularly effective within Iran. For example, Radio Farda has reached

15% of adults without an increase in funds since 2004; hiring Persian language broadcasters with

American accents lost credibility with Iranians; and hiring managers with very little knowledge

of Iranian culture and language is common.[48] Both companies must be overhauled to include

new management, increased budgetary spending, as well as hiring credible and reliable Iranian

dissidents living in America (now estimated to be the largest contingent in the world at over 200 million).[49] Perhaps entirely new programming has to be established under new names if it is determined that current operations no longer have credibility with Iranians.

Broadcasts through media outlets need to focus on regime weaknesses while discrediting the regime's propaganda sent to the citizens. The United States also must reach out to the oppressed minorities and youth to encourage them in their demonstrations in support of liberties and freedoms that are restricted by the current Islamic Republic administration. Information operations aimed at minorities and the youth may affect the outcome of the 2009 elections if a solid information operation campaign is developed. Placing blame on the regime for the recent economic sanctions against Iran will undermine the regime and cause the people to grow increasingly despondent with the leadership. As the elections draw near, reminding citizens about Ahmadinejad's failure to bring money to every household should give Ahmadinejad concern over his reelection. More importantly is to let the people of Iran know that America does not have any dilemmas with them; rather, the dilemma lies with the regime that oppresses citizen's freedoms and liberties.

America must be cautious to not back an individual candidate but rather back an ideology that represents freedom and change. America must also take advantage of Ahmadinejad's rhetoric concerning the 12th Imam's return, destruction of Israel, and nuclear weapons ambition. An astonishing 80% of Iranians favor full access to Iran's nuclear facilities and not develop nuclear weapons in return for external assistance. Also, 68% welcome normal trade relations with the United States.[50]

America's understanding of Iran is limited to the headlines Ahmadinejad receives for his various antics. News outlets need to saturate the channels with more information about Iran to educate the disenchanted in the United States. Political leadership, oppression, and dangers associated with Iran (e.g., nuclear ambition, terrorist ties) must be relayed to the American public. More importantly, America needs to be reassured that Iran is not, and will not become, another Iraq. American's must be reassured that every attempt to solve the Iranian problems are being made through other than military efforts, while at the same time letting Americans know the reasons that Iran cannot have nuclear weapons. With a better understanding of Iran's interests and desires, support for the use of military force will be tolerated IF all attempts were made at a peaceful resolution.

Oil, drugs, money, and war compound problems in Iran and are attributed to the strategic location of the plateau. The Iranian plateau can provide its citizens everything they need from profits gained from oil revenues. With oil prices at an all-time high and Iranian oil production ranking second in the world, 88% of Iranians believe this money should be used towards improving the economy and should be a government priority. In addition, Resolution 1737, sanctions against weapons of mass destruction suppliers to Iran and Resolution 1747, a broader restriction of 1737 and an imposition of a weapons-trade restriction with Iran are working in Iran. Many of Iran's trading partners, such as Germany, Japan (2006), and Italy (2007), are reducing their exports by seven, thirteen, and twenty percent respectively.[51] The US must apply international pressure to foreign countries who continue to trade with Iran to reduce the flow of imports to Iran. Keeping the economic vice on Iran will continue to separate the citizens from the government, but it is important to let the Iranian citizens know that the government, not the people, is to blame.

Military action against Iran will have devastating effects in America. Khamene'i stated that he would completely block the Strait of Hormuz if Iran was attacked (see Appendix F). This blockade can be a devastating blow to the American economy and world economy because it will raise the price of gasoline already to a record high since two-fifths of the world's seaborne oil passes through the Strait of Hormuz to foreign ports.[52] Strategically, block the Strait would be a good move for Iran as a last resort effort for its global effects, but would ultimately cause Iran's economy to collapse by exhausting Iran's 100-day oil reserve. America must maintain its presence in the Strait and defend the passage route with its superior navy.

Conclusion

The current presidential administration must diplomatically engage Iran concerning its nuclear weapons program and sponsorship of terrorist organizations. If Iran fails to engage in discussions, the U.S. must recognize and immediately take advantage of Iran's internal challenges while simultaneously applying diplomatic and further economic instruments of national power to further separate the Iranian government from its people. The U.S. government must apply information operations to educate and influence both Iranian and American populace and are the most important tools in the U.S. inventory. Military action against Iran must be used as a last resort and only after intelligence of nuclear weapons is confirmed with hard, concrete evidence. Pre-emptive strikes without a lack of intelligence will turn citizens against the U.S. and prolong the regime. The United States consistently allows Iranians time to further their nuclear ambitions while U.S. administrators contemplate military action. The U.S. will make a grave mistake financially, politically, and strategically if it takes military action in Iran without exhausting all other possible options beginning with diplomatic, informational, and economic actions towards the vulnerabilities of the Iranian people, politics, and plateau.